Review Tales

A Book Magazine For Indie Authors

Review Tales
A Book Magazine For Indie Authors

COPYRIGHT   2024
Review Tales Magazine - A Book Magazine for Indie Authors

Founder & Editor in Chief: S. Jeyran Main
Publisher: Review Tales Publishing & Editing Services
Print & Distribution: Ingram Spark
Designs: Pexels
ISBN 978-1-988680-52-1 (Paperback)
ISBN 978-1-988680-53-8 (Digital)
www.jeyranmain.com
For all inquiries, please contact us directly.

Contribitors

Donna Balon
Thomas T. Chin
Yona Katz
R. s. d'Arcy
Janet Stilson
Dagmara Sitek
Susan Dormady Eisenberg
CC Robinson
Andri E. Elia
David Rothman
Erna Buffie
John R. Miles
Graydon MCwilliams
Jason Lavender
Melody Horrill
Ann P Borrmann
Sophie Burrus-Muller
Steffanie Costigan
Tosca Lee
Fred G. Baker
Charlie Sheldon
Angela Van Breemen
Don Sawyer
L. A. Preston
Robert White
Beatriz M. Robles
Ali Master
Cheryl Kerr
John Edwards
Thad G. Long
Dr. Colleen Huber
John Landry
Charles McCormack
Howard Wolk

Photo Credits from Pexels:
Gabby K 5634667 p.2
Mlkbnl-7499773

Contents

Editor's Note

Dear Readers,

Welcome to the 12th edition of our magazine, a special fall release that celebrates the rich tapestry of indie authorship. As the leaves turn and the air grows crisp, we bring you a collection of insights, stories, and advice tailored to the heart and soul of every independent author.

This edition delves deep into the creative journey, featuring articles like "From Canvas to Pages: The Art of Becoming an Author" and "The Pen as Power: Writing as the Ultimate Revenge." We explore the transformative paths from poet to novelist, the cathartic power of book promotion, and the wisdom that seasoned authors have to share. Our pages are filled with book reviews, candid author confessions, and inspiration to fuel your writing journey.

As we celebrate this milestone of our 12th edition, we want to extend our deepest thanks to you, our dedicated readers. Your unwavering support has allowed this magazine to grow into a vibrant community of writers and readers alike. Together, we continue to champion the voices of indie authors, offering a platform for creativity, honesty, and the pursuit of literary dreams.

Thank you for being a part of our story. Here's to many more editions filled with the passion and power of indie writing.

Jeyran Main

Editor-in-Chief
Review Tales Magazine

Author Therapy During Book Promotion

Donna Balon

Book promotion can be lonely. I know the steps: activate social media accounts, schedule blog tours, and engage in author forums. Yet, book promotion is also an unexpected emotional journey.

I log in to my computer morning and night. How many books were sold? Are there any new reviews? What's the book's star rating?

Some days are exciting when sales are good. On no-sale days, I wonder whether I'm doing enough. There's a constant effort to garner positive reviews.

It's all new to me. What should I expect? My independence as a writer means I must seek my own therapy—author therapy.

Here are some ways I alleviate my book promotion anxieties:

Hobbies: Like many indie writers, I'm a crafter. I enjoy sewing and knitting. Working with my hands has been relaxing to take my mind off book marketing.

Blog Posts: I've searched the Internet for how to manage the disappointment of negative reviews. An old blog post provided a helpful answer: A negative review says more about the reviewer than the book.

I also found solidarity in learning about people's experiences in other artistic disciplines.

An Actor's Book: I found encouragement in the book by Jenna Fischer, the actress who played Pam Beesly on "The Office." In "The Actor's Life: A Survival Guide," Jenna shares how being part of the acting community advanced her career. Similarly, authors can find support in writer communities by engaging with other authors.

Reality Television: I'm a fan of the reality TV series "Project Runway," where fashion designers compete for a grand prize. Contestants speak of their love for designing and their dreams of success. Authors can relate to this passion. The judges' critiques are often frank and harsh, much like the honest reviews every author receives.

Indie authors are not only creative writers; we also need to be creative in finding therapeutic ways to maintain emotional strength while navigating the book promotion journey.

From Artist to Author

Thomas T. Chin

I have been an artist and art teacher for most of my professional life. Although I have always been interested in writing, becoming a book author was unexpected. Born in Beijing, China, I came to the United States to attend Bennington College, where I majored in fine arts, and creative writing was my second interest. I am an accomplished artist. One of my specialties is portrait painting, through which I have the opportunity to get to know many interesting people. My father, an editor-in-chief at Beijing Publishing House, initially influenced my interest in writing. He was also a book author himself.

Thomas Hardy's novels also had a major impact on my writing. I enjoyed his writing style.

What I find in common between art and writing is that both rely on observation. When I paint a landscape, I often work from memory and have a photographic memory. I enjoy people-watching, although I don't do this intentionally. My practice in observation and pre-visualization has helped me create the scenes in my book. Memories from people I have met and known have helped me develop my fictional characters.

Writing *Unpredictable Winds* was the result of a dream. One day, several years ago, I woke up with vivid images; I could even hear voices. It became clear then that what I "saw" in my dream should be a book. Within three days, I had the main plot of the book planned. Lee's character is based on my maternal grandfather, a successful businessman in Shanghai. And the Mei character was based on the housekeeper my family once had many years ago. *Unpredictable Winds* is a story of love, war, a secret, and an unintentional friendship that leads to devastating consequences.

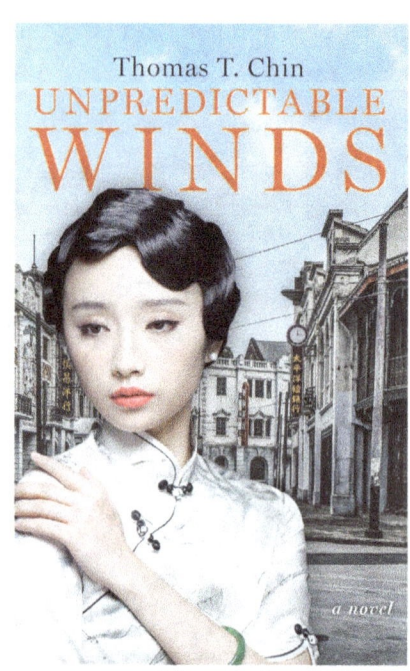

Never stop dreaming
Yona Katz

I grew up in a totalitarian society where not only people's lives and actions were controlled, but also their thoughts and even dreams. Individuality was a shame, being different was punishable, and anything less than perfection was rejected. I was very lucky to have had the opportunity to escape that suffocating world. Since leaving, I have lived in many countries, was exposed to many cultures, and learned a few languages (English is my fifth). Yet, even with my newfound freedom, I felt like a fledgling bird suddenly sprouting adult wings. I stumbled, fell, adapted, rose, and persisted.

I made much progress in shedding the remnants of my past indoctrination and personal trauma. However, the day I realized I was genuinely free was when, out of nowhere, the idea for a book formed in my head. I feverishly typed away for hours on end. Since then, writing has become my personal therapy and a means to reach the hearts of others. I want to let my readers know that embracing their uniqueness is acceptable but should be encouraged, that chasing perfection doesn't always lead to joy and that it's essential to consider all perspectives in any situation.

Personally, I am a very empathetic human being. I have much love and care to share. My goal in writing is to spread that love through inclusive novels with happy endings. I hope my readers will never give up reaching for the stars and stop dreaming.

The Long Way Around

R. S. d'Arcy

I have always loved reading and watching movies. I was enthralled with the creativity of someone doing something extraordinary outside their normal life or being in a completely different world or time. I never saw it as a career path. I was raised with the idea that you get a good job with benefits and save money for the future with a house, spouse, and kids. So, after college, I went to work for the Federal Government for the next twenty-plus years. I also took up the hobby of writing screenplays.

It all stopped as I moved up the ladder of upper management, leaving little time for writing. Then it all changed. I got the house, got married, lost my mother, and entered the world of a pandemic. I decided to seize upon the changes as an opportunity. Since my wife and I could not telework anywhere due to COVID-19, we moved from Long Island to Las Vegas. Shortly thereafter, I became a first-time dad at fifty. We decided that I would be the one to leave my job and become a stay-at-home parent rather than pay for a daycare provider. It turned into another opportunity. It gave me time to write again. Through the encouragement of my wife, I wrote my first book.

I independently published Sorcery & Sin in the Second World. It transported the reader to a fantasy world filled with swords, sorcery, and more. Rather than the main characters, a husband and wife, who have some specialized skills or superpowers, I made them like everyday people and saw how they navigate through a fantastical world. I hope the reader enjoys the journey as much as I have and escape for a few hours to a new world.

A Character in the Sci-Fi Thriller 'Universe of Lost Messages' Speaks Out

Janet Stilson

Hey. My name's Cheeta Lucida LaVera. You'll find me inside a new book by Janet Stilson called Universe of Lost Messages. She asked me to explain a few things.

First, you should know I'm 17, and I've seen some pretty nasty stuff. I was homeless on the streets of New York for a while. But I met a senator, Miles Morelli, who saved me. I became his assistant, and we had much fun building this robot in our spare time. Miles was going to help me pay for college and study robotics. That's what I love. It just about killed me when they reported that he died in a car accident.

After that, I was thrown into a metaverse—a virtual space called the Universe of Lost Messages. Instead of planets and stars, it's filled with millions of bubbles. Inside each one is a message. None of them reached the people that were supposed to get them. Crazy, right?

I was floating around there, really confused when I came across a message from the Senator that blew me away. He never died! Before he disappeared, Miles had investigated this secret political organization called The Fist and was going to blow their cover. So they put him in a private prison, along with some other people.

Two prisoners, Tristan and Izzie, have these superpowers of persuasion. The Fist wanted to use them to screw with people's heads all over the world. Those Fist people want to rule the whole planet.

Some messages in that Universe gave me clues about where that fricking prison might be. But I couldn't find it alone. I had to team up with some other people—like Izzie and Tristan's families—which is a real head trip, let me tell you.

Going through the Universe was like a tornado at times—crazy scary. But even though we were all desperate and determined to find the prison, some good things happened—really tight friendships, love, and the occasional laugh.

Loris Opens Up His Heart

Dagmara Sitek

In May 2023, a tragic event shook Poland deeply. A young boy called Kamilek from Czestochowa suffered severe abuse from his stepfather, leading to his hospitalization. Despite the tireless efforts of doctors, Kamilek's injuries were fatal, leaving the entire community in mourning.

The news of Kamilek's passing affected me deeply. How could someone hurt a vulnerable child like that? I couldn't stop thinking about it, so I started writing to help me deal with all those overwhelming feelings. That's how the Courage Tales series came to be.

I set out to honor the Polish boy's memory and amplify the voices of children like him—those who deal with troubled family environments. I wanted to create characters who reflected these children's inner strength and struggle, offering inspiration and teaching life lessons.

The main characters of the Courage Tales series, Inaya, Cam, and Loris, are children in foster care. I deliberately depicted them not as fantastical heroes but as real individuals confronting emotional challenges: anger, sadness, and loneliness. They find strength within their friendship, showcasing the transformative power of friendship and resilience.

"Loris Opens Up His Heart" is the first installment in my Courage Tales series. Through this beautifully illustrated book, I aim to instill hope in children. I want to remind them that amidst life's darkest moments, there are people who care deeply for them. I hope that Loris's journey, alongside his foster siblings, encourages young readers never to give up and to seek solace in the ongoing support of others.

Thinking about "Loris Opens Up His Heart," there are three important lessons children can take away:

> You are good enough.
> You are smart enough.
> You are brave enough.

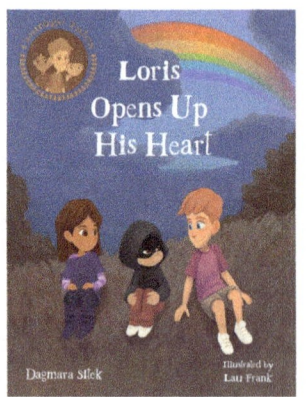

Reflecting on my journey following Kamilek's loss, I've come to appreciate the profound impact of self-reflection in growing my inner strength. While distractions like fun books and movies offer temporary respite, true growth comes from introspection and creative expression when times get tough.

My writing journey has been essential to my healing process. Likewise, I hope that "Loris Opens Up His Heart" serves as a ray of comfort and authenticity for children and their families. I hope it provokes self-reflection and self-discovery in children and empowers them to navigate challenges with courage and resilience.

Loris Opens Up His Heart is an uplifting but bittersweet story that was awarded the prestigious Mom's Choice Awards® Gold Recipient and is considered among the best products for families.

How I Wrote a Historical Novel That Combines Famous People with Fictional Characters

Susan Dormady Eisenberg

Every novel needs a dynamic protagonist and colorful secondary characters. To achieve this cast in my historical rom-com, One More Seat at the Round Table: A Novel of Broadway's Camelot, I mixed the legendary creators of this beloved 1960 musical—and the performers who gave it life—with characters of my invention.

How could I eliminate the personalities of those who made Camelot famous? Namely, Lerner and Loewe, the librettist and composer; Moss Hart, the director; Richard Burton, Julie Andrews, Roddy McDowall, and Robert Goulet, the stars. Without these luminaries, I would've had to dream up a fictional musical that would've lost Camelot's rich link to theater history.

Instead, I described the much-publicized backstage chaos when Camelot was out of town in previews, carefully researching how I portrayed the real people in my story. Richard Burton, for instance, was known for brilliant acting but also drinking and philandering, as mentioned in various memoirs. Thus, I felt safe to assign such peccadilloes to him. On the other hand, Julie Andrews sang gorgeously and acted well but was by all accounts a faithful wife to then-husband Tony Walton. And that's how I portrayed her.

To weave a compelling plot, I needed secondary characters who could interact freely with my invented protagonists, Jane Conroy, and Bryce Christmas, so I fictionalized several real cast members and backstage workers, borrowing their roles in the company while giving them new names and backgrounds. Thus, I had the leeway to develop situations that evoked tension and humor while giving my story the patina of truth.

And when I finished my final draft, I hired an intellectual property attorney to vet my manuscript. My careful sourcing impressed him, and he asked me to change a few details.

My advice to other writers is don't be afraid to include well-known people in your fiction. Please do your homework, limit your scope to what you know of their real personalities and behavior, and allow a literary attorney to review your book before publication.

As they say in show business, break a leg!

SUSAN DORMADY EISENBERG

ONE MORE SEAT AT THE ROUND TABLE

A NOVEL OF BROADWAY'S CAMELOT

Divided
by CC Robinson

When did you first realize you wanted to be a writer?

I don't remember a time when I haven't written. I was an imaginative child, composing stories for neighbors and friends and entertaining my family with made-up tales. I left fiction writing behind in my finance and, later in my medical career, trading fiction for non-fiction technical writing. It was only after my all-night dream of America after a devastating civil war fought over racial issues that my fiction-writing bug reawoke.

How do you schedule your life when you're writing?

I work part-time at our church, which I helped start, so juggling finance and pastoring duties as my writing life grew busier has been challenging. I dedicate entire days of the week to either writing or my part-time work. I'm more creative when I get into a focused zone for writing. I find this works the other way, as well. I'm more productive in my part-time position when I can dedicate all my energy to a day at a time.

Where did you get your information or idea for your book?

I had an all-night dream; maybe some would call it a nightmare. Our nation was in the middle of a civil war, an ethnic group fighting against ethnic groups in the cities, when our enemies took advantage of our division. Nuclear bombs destroyed both coasts and a large swath of the southern US, while an EMP (electromagnetic pulse bomb) knocked out the electricity across most of the US. Then, I saw four teenagers emerging from the devastation. They started out locked behind tall, impenetrable walls but joined together to bring freedom to the nation. I met my main characters, fully formed with all their mess and hope, toward the end of that dream. When I awoke, I knew I had to write Marcos's, Rose's, Harriet's, and Jason's stories. It has only been through working with an amazing developmental editor that now, ten years later, their story is forthcoming. Divided is a four-book series, one book for each of the main characters' stories.

What do you like to do when you're not writing?

When I'm not writing, I love being outside -- in the garden, swimming for fitness, hiking with my family, or riding around in my Jeep. My husband Steve and I also enjoy ballroom dancing, though we are skilled pros by no stretch of the imagination!

Author Interview

Healing of a Psychotherapist: A Journey of Rebellion, Redemption and Reflection
by Charles McCormack

When did you first realize you wanted to be a writer?

I never set out to be a writer; despite being published, I still don't consider myself one. A 'writer writes.' I only write when I need to get something out, which rarely happens. When it does, it's like I'm pregnant. Writing is the midwife, helping me get my thoughts and feelings out and onto paper where I can look at them, think about them, and rewrite them again and again until I feel that it is saying what I wanted to say all along but didn't have the words for it until I put the effort in.

How do you schedule your life when you're writing?

I only write when I feel like it, but when I do, the writing becomes all-consuming and takes over my life; it becomes very selfish. I enter a trance state of intense focus, and everything else disappears. I often miss meals and appointments with my patients because I lost all sense of time. Boy, was that embarrassing. I've learned to set an alarm.

What would you say is your interesting writing quirk?

I think the losing myself in the writing to the exclusion of almost everything else is my most interesting writing quirk.

How did you get your book published?

My first book, Treating Borderline States in Marriage, was published by Jason Aronson Publishers, now part of Random House. It was sponsored by the Director of the Washington School of Psychiatry to Jason Aronson, who was interested in compiling a library of psychoanalytically oriented books. The current book, Healing of a Psychotherapist, is self-published. I desired complete control over the book and valued the ability to rewrite and republish it several times before shaping it into its final form.

Where did you get your information or idea for your book?

My inspiration for the book came when my son asked about life; I initially said happiness but found it unconvincing. I began writing to explore this idea further. Then, my daughter requested a book about me for our grandchildren. Instead of a list of favorites, I transformed it into a narrative of my life's challenges, lessons, and personal growth. As I wrote, the idea evolved into something more significant, resonating with the human condition. Writing became a therapeutic journey, delving deep into vivid memories and unresolved emotions. It became a space for laughter, tears, and profound self-reflection.

Lelya Dorche and the Coney Island Cure
by David Rothman

When did you first consider yourself a writer?

Oh, I haven't a clue! As a child, I was enthralled with a love for reading and writing from as far back as I can remember. My earliest memories are of four or five-year-old me lazing on a beach chair on the Jersey Shore with my eyes glued to the pages of a children's book as I listened to the waves fall. Heaven on earth! When I was seven, my family suffered a horrible tragedy. My ten-year-old sister was hit by a car and died. My whole world fell apart. I lost myself in my huge collection of fairy tales, and I began to keep a diary. Reading and writing saved me. As a young adult, I wrote an awful lot of bad poetry. When I turned to the short story format and got published, I started calling myself a writer

How do you schedule your life when you're writing?

We're all busy with jobs, family, and all kinds of curve balls life throws our way. I was fortunate to land a full-time faculty position teaching writing for the City University of New York (CUNY). I have Fridays off to write and three months that are completely mine each summer!

What would you say is your interesting writing quirk?

I sometimes start writing sessions on a bench in a deserted park, where I interview myself out loud about the piece I am working on.

Where did you get your idea for your book?

In late March 2020, as the first wave of the pandemic descended on New York City, I crept cautiously back into my apartment building from the local grocery store. As I approached the stairwell, I caught the stare of a neighbor hiding behind the mailbox wall. She had a look of terror in her eyes. She stared at my hands as if they held seven bloody claws. I knew her well enough to know that her young daughter had a respiratory issue, an underlying condition, that is. And here I was, bringing deadly germs back from the public market. As I hurried away up the lonely staircase, all I could think was that we could use a little magic in our world right about now. And so, I started composing Lelya Dorche and the Coney Island Cure.

What do you like to do when you're not writing?

I'm a drummer in a NYC rock band. I find that writing and percussion have a lot in common. It's all about getting into a groove and finding the pacing. I'd say that goes for cooking as well!

Let Us Be True
by Erna Buffie

When did you first realize you wanted to be a writer?

I was eleven or twelve when I read my first "grown-up" book, Richard Llewellyn's novel How Green Was My Valley, and I think that may have been the first time I imagined myself becoming a writer. Set in a small Welsh mining town in the 19th century, I found the book so moving, and I was so completely swept away to another time and place and engaged in the lives of a family so different from my own that when I turned the last page, I distinctly remember thinking, I'd like to write a book like that one day.

I took a rather circuitous route to that goal, becoming first a writer and director for the documentary film, but, in the end, I circled back to fiction, using the storytelling skills I'd learned in the film to write my first novel, Let Us Be True.

How did you get your book published?

When my book was more or less finished, I decided to attend the Sagehill Writers' Workshop. The writer directing the sessions was one of my favorite Canadian authors, Helen Humphreys, and I wrote to her beforehand to ask if she would have time to read my manuscript during the 10-day workshop. She agreed, and the results were incredibly encouraging.

Not only was she keen to see Let Us Be True get published, but she also gave me invaluable advice, suggesting that I send the book to midsized publishers first, as debut authors sometimes get lost in the shuffle at big publishing houses. So, I submitted the manuscript to several smaller publishers and was lucky enough to be picked up by the second one. Of course, the fact that the book also came with a recommendation from Helen was a huge plus.

What do you like to do when you're not writing?

I'm always writing! Sometimes on a documentary film, but these days, more often than not, I can be found writing opinion pieces for my local newspaper, usually on urban environmental issues. Readers can find a lot of those articles on my blog: https://www.ernabuffie.com/

I also volunteer with a local group fighting to preserve and expand Winnipeg's urban forest as part of a climate resiliency effort. And when I'm not writing, volunteering, or appearing before the city council, I love being at my little lake cottage with my Shih Tzu, Olly, and partner, Brian.

Passion Struck
by John R. Miles

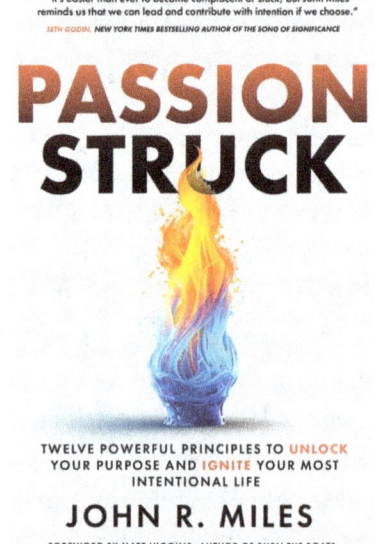

When did you first realize you wanted to be a writer?

I first realized my calling to be a writer in my 30s amidst a busy life balancing senior executive responsibilities and raising a family. I've always been captivated by the magic of storytelling—its power to forge connections, stir emotions, and spark change. My foray into writing was a seamless extension of my deep-seated love for communication and my ambition to profoundly impact the lives of others.

Initially, my writing served as a personal sanctuary—a space to sift through experiences, flesh out ideas, and share the wisdom gleaned from my roles in leadership, coaching, and public speaking. It wasn't until I assumed the role of Associate Publisher and Editor-in-Chief at Bold Business that my passion for writing truly took flight.

The leap from personal musings to becoming a published author was fueled by the realization that the lessons I've learned—especially those from overcoming adversity and committing to a life of intention—could profoundly touch and uplift others. This revelation birthed "Passion Struck," a synthesis of my life's stories, rigorous research, and enlightening discussions with luminaries across diverse fields.

Writing then transformed for me; it became more than just self-expression—it became a mission to empower others to unleash their potential and embrace lives marked by purpose, passion, and authenticity.

How do you schedule your life when you're writing?

While I don't write full-time, my role as the founder of Passion Struck keeps me deeply engaged in creating transformative content. This includes hosting the Passion Struck podcast, where I engage with thought leaders to share personal and professional growth insights. Additionally, I develop courses, conduct workshops, and deliver keynote speeches aimed at empowering individuals to lead intentional lives.

Balancing these responsibilities requires meticulous planning. I carve out dedicated blocks in my daily writing routine, weaving it seamlessly alongside podcast management, social media engagement, and content preparation for speaking engagements. This disciplined approach ensures I stay productive and focused on inspiring others to embrace lives driven by purpose, resilience, and personal growth.

What would you say is your interesting writing quirk?

One of my intriguing writing quirks is how I use physical movement to overcome writer's block and ignite my creativity. Whether it's a brisk walk, a spin class, or some light stretching, getting my body in motion awakens my mind and enhances the flow of ideas. This practice re-energizes me and allows me to approach challenges with renewed perspectives, fueling my creativity and productivity when I return to writing. By integrating physical activity into my writing process, I blend creativity's physical and mental dimensions, keeping my body and narrative dynamically engaged.

Additionally, I have a special affinity for my coffee cup—it's not just any cup; it's a super awesome, insulated one in a vibrant blue with a comfortable handle that I cherish. While it's not extravagant, having it by my side enhances my writing experience.

Either Peace or War
by Graydon MCwilliams

What would you say is your interesting writing quirk?

My finer point was that I had a story of action, romance, tragedy, and comedic relief. I know how to punch the button at the end of a chapter.

How did you get your book published?

I paid ten grand for a publisher and editor.

Where did you get your information or idea?

I fucking lived it for two years. I walked and breathed through the story and spent fifteen years figuring out how I wanted to present it. Once I understood how much I could embellish what happened to make someone understand the story's emotion, the novel wrote itself every night I sat down.

Is there anything you would like to confess as a writer?

I hate that writers compete. Artists should help each other. Most "writers" haven't had an original thought. They reword what they've read or heard off social media. I feel like I'm battling the ones with inspirational regurgitation. People who want to be writers don't seem to understand how much time writers put into creation. Why hasn't anyone warned them that art is an addiction?

How do you process and deal with negative book reviews?

I only have one negative book review, and I text him when I read it. "You bastard! You got me SO good! Seeing your name next under a one-star review had me rolling." Even then, I don't care. It's published. The work is done, and most commentators will do nothing more than talk until there's a new subject to discuss.

The Sad Giraffe
by Jason Lavender

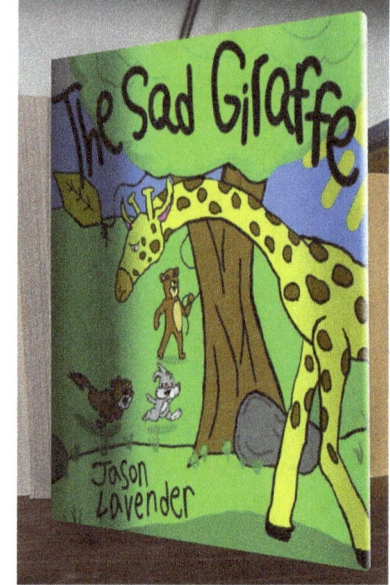

When did you first realize you wanted to be a writer?

I have had an interest in writing since before I can remember. When I was younger, I would play with toys, my favorite being Legos, and I would make up backstories and battle scenes for all of my many characters. This then transferred to school when I would have creative writing projects and go above and beyond and fill entire pages with overly detailed stories way over the required page count, much to the dismay of the teachers to decipher all of my essays. I was never good at punctuation. Additionally, I would constantly draw, creating many worlds on the pages. So naturally, I combined both worlds and started making picture books.

How do you schedule your life when you're writing?

I am very new to writing so I have to have it as my side hobby for now. I soon hope to do it full time but right now I work in the mornings and then get straight to creative activities. If I don't feel very inspired that day, I will do something that will make my brain work like arts and crafts and think about what I should do next in my book.

What would you say is your interesting writing quirk?

My interesting quirk is that I like to draw the situation before I write it. It helps me visualize it better than I can put it into words.

How did you get your book published?

First, I wrote and illustrated it. Then, I emailed and applied to all the places I could that would publish children's books. Some gave offers. Then I choose the best one.

Where did you get your information or idea for your book?

I had always been disappointed in the children's books I would read at Barnes and Noble. The lack of artistry and story in them made me feel like I could do better. So, I originally drew out a skeleton of the story on my random paper. The entire story just came to me. It wasn't really inspired by anything but my own mind. When quarantine struck, I had nothing to do but write or draw. My parents got me a new tablet with an art program where I finally digitized it to eventually be submitted to Kirkhouse.

What do you like to do when you're not writing?

When not writing, I can be consumed in my other hobbies, such as drawing, skating, and climbing trees with friends; I hope to make a career out of climbing things one day. Or entertaining my girlfriend.

A Cat Called Q and the Magic Globe
by Melody Horrill

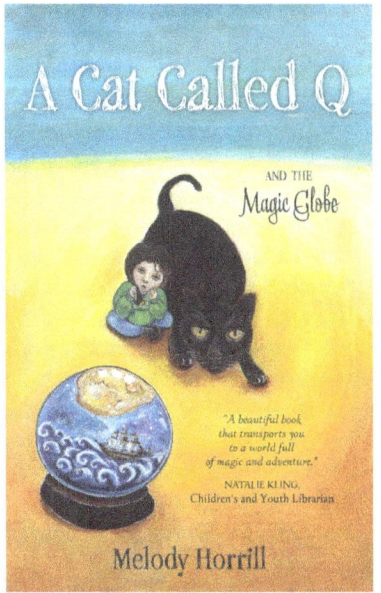

When did you first realize you wanted to be a writer?

I always loved reading as a child – it was a way for me to escape the domestic violence in my family home. I would often sit for hours nestled in a tree or a bush, delving into picture books and fantastical tales. However, it was only in my later years that I felt I had enough experience and confidence to attempt writing a book.

How do you schedule your life when you're writing?

I tend to clear my head and go for a walk along the beach before I attempt any writing. I set aside 3 to 4 hours, close the door of my spare bedroom, and make sure my rescue cat is seated by my side. He is very much my literary muse!

What would you say is your interesting writing quirk?

I've been told I have a knack for bringing scenes to life. I think I've been able to do that because I worked for years in broadcast television and always wrote scripts for footage and images. I use the same technique, but the 'footage' or 'images' are in my mind these days.

What do you like to do when you're not writing?

I love spending time at the beach or out in nature. It invigorates me and reminds me of the reason I write! I also love spending time creating in the kitchen. Cooking is a little like writing – you put many ingredients together and create something from it … hopefully it works, but sometimes it doesn't!

How do you process and deal with negative book reviews?

It's difficult. As a writer, you hope others will enjoy your work, but I've come to accept that I cannot please everyone. I think as long as you're satisfied that you've done the best job you can do – then that must be enough. I have learned a great deal since writing my memoir and have taken on some of the criticisms I received and learned from them – so it can be turned around to a positive.

Chester The Almost Pirate
by Ann P Borrmann

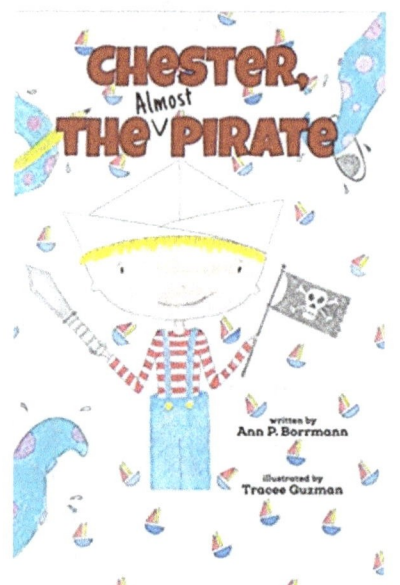

When did you first realize you wanted to be a writer?

I never thought about becoming a writer at all - until my granddaughter was born in October 2019.

During a heavy rain storm, her father's sailboat was washed away. I thought that I would write a little story about that incident and self-publish it under the title, The Jolly Bupbup, as a gift to her (of course, in that story, Bubbup finds her sailboat and has tea with Twinkles, so it all ends better for the jolly Bubbup than it did for my son in law whose boat was never found, and who did not have tea with any Twinkles.) That story, in 2020, was the beginning. From there, it just morphed into something I enjoyed doing.

While I have had three more grandchildren since 2019, and I will dedicate a book to each one, I try to write fun stories that generally appeal to all children. Chester the (almost) Pirate was written in 2022 with my grandson in mind because I think all little boys (maybe some girls) go through a pirate stage. I turned Chester into a fun 2-book series, with the second book, Never Take a Pirate's Pearls, having come out in 2023.

How do you schedule your life when you're writing?

I am a Grade 5/6 teacher at a small private school, so I have almost three months off in the summer when I can work -if and when inspiration strikes! It's a little more tricky during the school year, obviously. However, the first thing in the morning is usually when I have the best ideas and do my best writing. Maybe I can do it more full-time when I retire, but for now, it's as I can.

What would you say is your interesting writing quirk?

I don't know if this is so much a writing quirk as it is a writing necessity! But I have found that when I write a story, I tweak it and get it so I am happy with it, then I leave it alone and let it "rest" for 4-6 months, and when I come back to it later on, I usually think 'yep, that's pretty bad!' and do a major overhaul on it! First drafts are never good - at least not for me!

Also I tend to work on a couple of stories at a time, flipping back and forth between them.

How did you get your book published?

I wrote Chester, the (almost) Pirate before I got an agent, so I queried it myself too many different publishers who would accept manuscripts without an agent. I have never heard back from most of them, but it only takes one publisher who likes your story! Interestingly, the same week I received a contract from Lawley for Chester, the (almost) Pirate, I got a response from an agent (for a different book, since sold to Ever Imagine Press.) Needless to say, that was a great week!

...And Why Not?
by Sophie Burrus- Müller

When did you first realize you wanted to be a writer?

In my 20s, while going through a significant life learning curve, I realized that I wanted to write a book that could help people. I didn't know what the topic would be at that time, but I felt deep down that it was a project I wanted to include on my bucket list. I waited 15 years before writing my first book, but it was definitely worth it, and I look forward to continuing my writing journey.

How do you schedule your life when you're writing?

Now, writing is a bit like painting. You can sit in front of your canvas or blank page, but if your good friend, inspiration, is not there with you, well... there is not much you will get done. If it is a week where I feel I have good ideas percolating inside my head, I jot them down and try to organize my time so I can give myself three hours of uninterrupted time in the following days to sit and get some work done.

How did you get your book published?

I decided to go down the self-publishing route. I was very clear as to what I wanted my first book to be and how I wanted it to look. Once I wrote the first draft, I searched for an editor who helped me polish the text and format the book so it could be published in print and as an e-book. Then, I would say the real work began in finding different ways to market the book and get it out there.

Where did you get your information or idea for your book?

In 2021, I made a big change in my life, and after about a year, at 4 in the morning one day, the light bulb inside my head just lit. From that moment, I knew I wanted to share my life experience and key learnings with others who might be hitting a crossroads in their life and need some comfort or guidance.

What do you like to do when you're not writing?

I like to paint. Painting is my meditation. It is such a soothing process and, funnily enough, inspires me to write. Creativity brings in more creativity!

What was one of the most surprising things you learned in creating your book?

All the time was spent researching how to get the book self-published and marketed. There is just so much information out there, and there is no one best way to do it. Loads of sites and services promise best-seller status and great sales if you work with them, but when you dig a bit further, you realize there is no such thing. Writing the book is fun; getting it out there will be a game of time, perseverance and a good marketing strategy and budget.

Land of the Dragon
by Steffanie Costigan

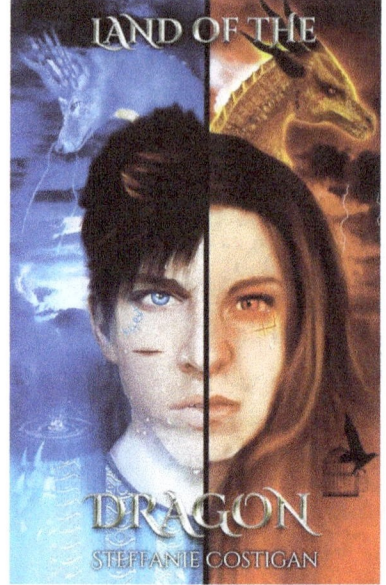

When did you first realize you wanted to be a writer?

Honestly, I have been writing ever since I was very young so it's something I've always had a desire to be.

How do you schedule your life when you're writing?

As a journalist/reporter and mommy of four, I must be organized, as you can imagine. I have a schedule book I carry around with me, but with that said, I also must be flexible when things don't go as planned. I have a very supportive husband that helps me out tremendously. On a good day after work, I can get two hours' worth of writing in.

What would you say is your interesting writing quirk?

One of my quirks is when I develop a character, I create them around a personality type and make them make decisions in my writing based on their personality type.

What do you like to do when you're not writing?

When I am not writing, I am writing for my local paper. I also love to draw or paint. If I'm not doing art, I enjoy spending time with my family and kids.

As a child, what did you want to do when you grew up?

I have always wanted to be a writer and publish books, but there was one point where I wanted to be a lawyer as I enjoyed participating in debates.

How do you process and deal with negative book reviews?

I have not had one yet, luckily, although I was a little sad when my five-star streake was broken with a 4 star. I just shared my thoughts and feelings with another friend who is more senior than I am in the writing industry. It was nice to express myself, get good encouragement, and hear my friend's experience with negative comments on reviews she has encountered.

Where did you get your information or idea for your book?

Research and from my dreams I have had while sleeping.

Is there anything you would like to confess about as an author?

Um, I don't know... I am Scorpio. So, I don't know if that plays a part in my writing.

Demon
by Tosca Lee

Demon: A Memoir just released in its fourth edition. What does this mean to you?

I'm super excited for this book to be back out in the world in an all-new fourth edition—both it and my second novel, Havah: The Story of Eve, which is also re-releasing in a new fourth edition on August 13. For me, it's both humbling and gratifying to see how many readers revisit Demon: A Memoir and to hear from those who recommend it to their friends. I am deeply moved by the letters I receive and the personal stories readers share with me. It's an incredible honor to have my story become a part of someone else's life. Given that it took six years for Demon to be picked up by its first publisher in 2006, it truly feels like a miracle. This book is special to me not only because of that but also because it's the one that launched my career.

What's changed since the first edition?

The story remains the same, with a few technology updates (when I initially wrote *Demon,* like the main character Clay, I owned a flip phone) and some very minor tweaks. I can't help it—I've made small adjustments to one sentence or another every time a new edition has come out. Something brand new for this edition is that *Demon* (and *Havah,* too) is now available for the very first time in hardcover. These are the only two of my books that haven't been released in hardcover, and it's so nice to finally offer longtime fans that option. It only took 17 years, but better late than never, right?

In addition to the hardcover, *Demon* and *Havah* both feature gorgeous new cover art, trivia about the story, and discussion questions, and *Havah* even includes bonus chapters.

You get asked regularly for a sequel to Demon: A Memoir. Will we see it become a series?

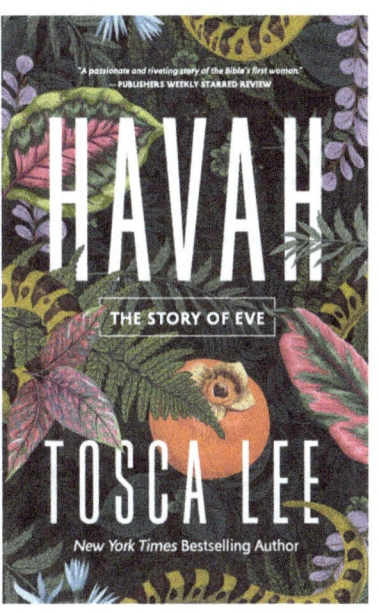

I get asked this a lot, but I've always felt that the story ended as it should, so I don't have any plans to write a follow-up. However, I never say "never."

WORDS OF WISDOM ABOUT WRITING THE GREAT AMERICAN NOVEL

Fred G. Baker

I haven't reached those heady heights yet, but try reading the truly great works of others, such as F. Scott Fitzgerald's The Beautiful and Damned. There is something comforting in that novel that contains such creative and wonderful prose. It shows me what talent I can achieve even if my meager scribbling doesn't reach that level. (Not yet, anyway. I still hope to improve.) When I attended my first writing conference, (I don't go to many—expensive, and most are directed toward novice writers. Better to save the funds for my editors.) I was awed by the authors I met who had written many books and had a strong reader following. I asked one fellow how to get started and get published. He had his own words of wisdom. He said to find the genre I wanted to work in and read the top one hundred books in that line.

He said I should then pick one whose style I liked and then copy that style. That way, I would find a niche within the market. I thanked him, but upon consideration, that was not for me. I didn't want to copy someone else. I wanted to be more creative than that. Of course, you learn a lot by reading other authors and what worked for them in plot, style, voice, and so on. And, of course, you want to learn what works in that field. But I didn't want to be a copycat. How could I be creative if so constrained?

My words of wisdom are to read outside your genre as much as possible, including some literary works, if you wish to elevate your writing and make your work stand out from the crowd of authors in one genre. Only then will you develop your own voice and style. If your job catches on with an audience, then you will be successful on your own terms and not as an also-ran.

Fred G. Baker is a hydrologist, historian, and writer living in Colorado. He writes fiction and non-fiction books and articles. He specializes in the genres of science fiction/fantasy, mystery/espionage, and thrillers. He is the author of _An Imperfect Crime, Desert Sanctuary, Desert Underworld, Einstein's Raven, Zona: The Forbidden Land, Life, Death, and Espionage, The Black Freighter, and the Modern Pirate Series_ of short and long stories. For more information, please see his website: othervoicespress.com.

WRITING A SERIES....
Charlie Sheldon

Writing a trilogy is different than writing a single book. My Strong Heart Series started as a single book. Then I wrote a second, Adrift, from material deleted from Strong Heart. Then, I needed to write further to wrap up some unresolved issues from the first tales. I faced a critical decision - do I write the books as stand-alone tales or not? How do I link stand-alone tales into one trilogy? Stand-alone books mean a reader can pick up any book and find it alone, satisfying, and complete. Most trilogies are not stand-alone. They offer summaries or backstories, and a reader has to start with the first book.

With Totem, the third tale in the series, I wrote basically two books in one: a long, deep, rich tale that concluded the trilogy and one that, were a reader to choose it first, might then draw a reader into the first two tales. It is hard to write separate but linked tales with many of the same characters without offering extensive backstories or repeatedly introducing characters already seen. My choice has been to define the characters by their actions, letting their backstories emerge with events as the reader proceeds. Of course, it is best, deepest, and richest to read the trilogy in order - Strong Heart, Adrift, Totem - but at the same time, some readers like discovering this world and people in Adrift or Totem and then looping back to Strong Heart to flesh out the full tale.

These tales, and Totem especially, offer a world, place, and people based on current reality but with a touch of magic realism. In the end, this world and its events required a trilogy structure. I can only hope readers agree.

Charlie Sheldon spent 15 years in the commercial fishing industry as a deckhand, mate, skipper and consultant, then worked at various Ports for 28 years before returning to sea in 2012 as a merchant sailor. In 1988, he wrote his first novel, Fat Chance, and he has written several since. Since 1990, he has lived in the Pacific Northwest. The Strong Heart Series emerged from his experiences hiking Olympic National Park, working with various Puget Sound Tribes, and years at sea. He attended Yale University and the University of Massachusetts, and he holds an MS in Wildlife Biology.

TRANSFORMATION FROM POET TO FICTION WRITER

Angela van Breemen

My journey as a writer began early when I discovered the power of words. As in all families, parents will argue on occasion. I remember sitting my ten-year-old self down at my little desk and writing my first poem, instinctively knowing the words would provide solace. Afterward, I presented my handwritten poem to my mom and dad; their expressions softened, and my mother, with tears in her eyes, told me everything was okay. This lesson taught me the magic of words and how poetry can portray emotion and imagery in a succinct and powerful way.

In the years that followed, I continued to write poetry but never gave serious thought to writing a book. I had made a half-hearted attempt in my early twenties when I first developed the plot for Past Life's Revenge, but I allowed life's demands to distract me. I placed the unfinished manuscript in a drawer, where it stayed for nearly four decades.

In December of 2022, while going through my desk, I came across the yellowed and curled pages of the manuscript. This time, I sat down, read it, and realized it had the makings of a great story and that I had to complete it. Once I made the decision, the excuses and the barriers I had set for myself as a younger person evaporated, and I began to write.

The psychics I had met while growing up influenced me profoundly, and the concepts of reincarnation and spiritualism flowed into my novel effortlessly. I suspect the years of not writing this book were not as inactive as I thought. I never stopped asking questions such as, what if someone was murdered, and what if they reincarnated so soon after death that they would encounter their killer again in their current life? What would they do? It's these questions my protagonist, David Harris, faces.

Writing the book and seeing it in print was a terrific and satisfying experience. So much so that I am busy working on the second book in the David and Harris Emma Jackson mystery series!

Angela van Breemen, a University of Guelph graduate in management economics, co-owned a dental supply company before focusing on writing, music, and volunteering at a wildlife rehabilitation center. She authored her first novel, Past Life's Revenge, a crime thriller with a spiritual twist, and is an active member of the Wordsmiths Writers' Group, Crime Writers of Canada, and South Simcoe Arts Council. A Soprano Soloist, Angela released her debut album In The Breeze in 2024, featuring original Celtic music based on her poetry. She lives in Loretto, Ontario, with her husband, author Peter Thomas Pontsa.

WRITING AS REVENGE

Don Sawyer

Years ago, I attended a writers' conference where a speaker made a comment that stayed with me. "With writing," he told us, "you can always exact revenge, no matter how long ago the wrongs. Writing becomes a means of getting even."

Now, writing about a wretched teacher I had when I was in Grade 2 to "exact revenge" is not exactly in the same league as detailing the horrors of the Odessa pogrom from which the speaker's grandfather had fled. However, vengeance was still at the heart of my Miss Flint stories.

Creating, recreating, and embellishing a monster from my past that I could take out my frustration on -- and then share with my sympathetic daughters as bedtime stories -- became quite satisfying. I started with

some actual stories about the Meanest Teacher in the World, but unlike in my versions, I had no vengeful comrades, and I kept my anger and sadness to myself. But, as noted, it's never too late for revenge. Miss Flint became increasingly villainous, and my stories inevitably ended with what I would have liked to have happened.

So that's how they began -- a smidgen of a recalled true story elaborated with creative ways to wreak vengeance on Miss Flint, the embodiment of the repressive teacher, the thoughtless, uncomprehending adult, the soul-squashing representative of the oligarchy. An actual horseback ride, museum visit, and school picnic were the kernel of recalled school days that provided the platform for elaborately contrived plots by my 2nd-grade cohorts and me. Sure, we had to endure a certain amount of humiliation and mistreatment, but we didn't have to take it sitting down.

Revenge is sweet, no matter how long deferred.

Don is an educator and writer who grew up in Michigan and moved to Canada in the 1960s. After leaving his PhD program in Modern Chinese History at the University of British Columbia, he embraced a variety of teaching roles across the globe, from Newfoundland to West Africa, British Columbia, and Jamaica. These diverse experiences have shaped his writing, resulting in over 12 books, including the Canadian bestsellers *Where the Rivers Meet* and *Tomorrow Is School and I Am Sick to the Heart Thinking about It*. Don has also contributed articles and op-eds to many journals and major Canadian newspapers. After living and working in Salmon Arm, BC for over 30 years, he now resides in St. Catharines, Ontario, with his wife of 54 years, Jan Henig Sawyer.

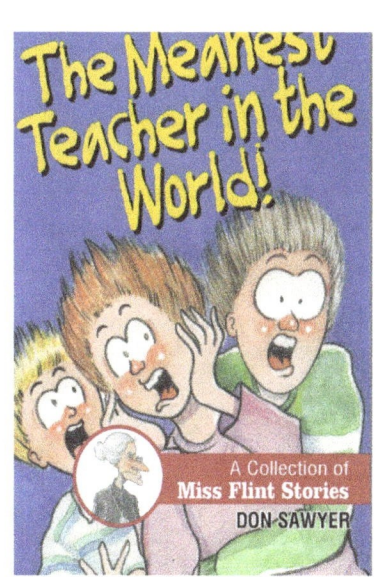

CAN A SYMPATHETIC PERSONALITY SIGNAL STRENGTH?

L. A. Preston

Why do some people view being kind, loving, and sympathetic as being 'soft'? Why do more introverted individuals, including young adults, become bullied or experience extensive mocking, whether at work, at home, or on social media? Is it because those people are not 'soft' after all but brave enough to express their uniqueness and kinder qualities that tend to flow in direct opposition to modern perceptions of the 'norm'?

In my book, 'Doctrine of the Asurlette- Fair's Onyx,' which is book one in a projected series of five books, one of the protagonists, General Dieter Llanfair, is the Asurlette's bravest first lieutenant on the pre-physical plane of Ped-Carreg. The kind-hearted Dieter comes to the aid of brother and sister Onyx and Sionen Cattarini, but in doing so,

contravenes his orders. He is the most courageous person in Llanfair. He is willing to sacrifice his own destiny to be with his beloved Kamille rather than abandon or hound the two innocent children, yet still suffers abuse from his peers in the form of mocking (from the fire dragoons) and denigration from Reverend Kalinowski, who thinks that Dieter's willingness to help others is a sign of evil in disguise rather than a force for good.

The minister's unkind outburst is a direct consequence of his inaccurate assumptions that Dieter must be a harmful influence because he is different (unique) due to his genuinely kind nature being coupled with his extreme height, seemingly eccentric style of clothing, unusual hair and, most importantly, his ability to convey his feelings easily. Although all of these attributes are positive, people generally feel more at ease with what they understand from a personal perspective, so they become suspicious or offensive if they cannot compute another person's individual traits.

An excerpt from chapter nineteen, 'The Professor's Quest,' of some aerial writing within a cloud of cyanobacteria says, 'yet do you linger at the sight of beauty or grace, or solely the noxious unimportance of one's own nauseating disillusion?'

The only weak and unattractive person is not the one who shows sympathy but causes hurt through words or deeds.

Lisa, 58, lives in West Glamorgan, South Wales, with her husband, Robert, and daughter, Charlotte. She assists with her husband's home-based business while training as a Reiki practitioner. Lisa holds a Diploma in Clinical Aromatherapy and studied Phytotherapy (Herbal Medicine) through distance learning. Her first Young Adult novel, *Doctrine of the Asurlette - Fair's Onyx*, is the beginning of a five-book series, with the second book currently in progress.

SUMMARY OF FADE TO BLACK

Robert White

In White's collection of 22 noir tales, the "unholy trinity" of greed, lust, and revenge drives the characters into dark and desperate situations. Each story is a gritty exploration of how these motives intertwine, often leading to tragic outcomes. In "Gone Fishing," a man is lured into dangerous waters by his best friend after an affair with his wife. In "Marigold's Diner," a thief on the run from a botched casino heist finds his fate altered by a roadside waitress. "Barn Find" follows a thief who stumbles upon a decaying muscle car in a barn, leading to a dangerous heist. Other tales include a debt collector in "Fish Out of Water," an ex-con reliving his past in "Kiss of Death," and a man discovering a kidnapped girl in "A Package

for Delivery." Stories like "Kettle Blowing" and "Perfect Stranger" feature ordinary men facing extraordinary threats. The settings are as bleak as the characters' lives—sleazy motels, seedy diners, and shadowy bars. In "Revenge of the Judas Goat," a disgruntled ex-employee seeks vengeance on a California highway, while "Missed Call" tells of a woman's deadly game with a new lover.

Though most characters in *Fade to Black* find themselves running toward their doom, a few stories offer a glimmer of hope. In "The One Who Saves You," a young lawyer's fall from grace leads to an unexpected friendship in a homeless camp. Meanwhile, "The Soul Food King of Indianapolis" and "Boosting for the Devil" reveal the harsh realities of life and the consequences of breaking the rules.

The collection closes with "I Remember," where a sociopathic con manipulates an ambitious listener, proving that in White's world, fate is as unforgiving as the characters themselves.

Robb T. White is a Derringer-nominated fiction writer from Northern Ohio who has published crime, noir, and hardboiled novels as well as dozens of genre stories in various magazines, websites, and anthologies. His crime thriller The Russian Heist was named by Thriller Magazine as winner in the Best Novel category for 2020. The crime story "Inside Man" was selected for Best American Mystery Stories 2019 (Houghton-Mifflin, 2020). Private-eye Raimo Jarvi appeared in Northtown Eclipse and Northtown Blitz, both by Fahrenheit Press, U.K. Jade Hui, Special Agent, made her first appearance in Perfect Killer (Crowood Press, 2018), a thriller cited by the British website Murder, Mayhem & More as a finalist for its Top Ten Crime Books of the year. A collection of seventeen revenge tales, Betray Me Not, was selected by the Independent Fiction Alliance as a Truly Best Independent Book of 2022.

ARTWORDS
Beatriz M. Robles

Reviewer: Jeyran Main

Artwords by Beatriz M. Robles is a mesmerizing collection that showcases the author's unique ability to blend words with visual art, creating a fascinating exploration of language. Robles arranges words to form shapes and pictures through calligrams, transforming simple phrases into captivating images. But the book goes beyond calligrams; Robles skillfully manipulates text from other works, highlighting specific terms to craft her prose. The interplay between everyday objects, such as scissors and sponges, with stories and sensual language gives the texts multiple layers of meaning.

The book is a poetic journey where each piece carries an implicit message or clever wordplay, resulting in a tapestry of narratives that can amuse, confuse, or deeply resonate with the reader. Robles' creativity shines through on every page, making *Artwords* a delightful surprise for those who appreciate the intelligent use of language.

One of the book's standout aspects is how Robles incorporates photographs that merge literature with ordinary objects. These images capture the simplicity and casual nature of daily life, adding a tangible connection to the abstract beauty of her prose. For instance, a photograph of a comb paired with words creates a scene where a woman speaks to her comb about how it boosts her confidence—a simple yet profound interaction. Additionally, the author's metaphors about sex and intimacy cleverly unite words and pictures to form short, thought-provoking narratives that evoke laughter and reflection.

Artwords is exceptionally well-edited, with no noticeable errors throughout. Robles employs straightforward language, making her compositions accessible to a wide audience. This simplicity enhances the reader's understanding and fosters a closer connection between the author and her audience.

Artwords is a brilliant collection that seamlessly blends the sensual elements of everyday life with creative visual expressions. I highly recommend this book to adult readers interested in sensual poetry, calligrams, and other word-based art forms. However, those who prefer to avoid themes of intimacy or are not inclined towards poetry or artistic prose may not find this book to their taste.

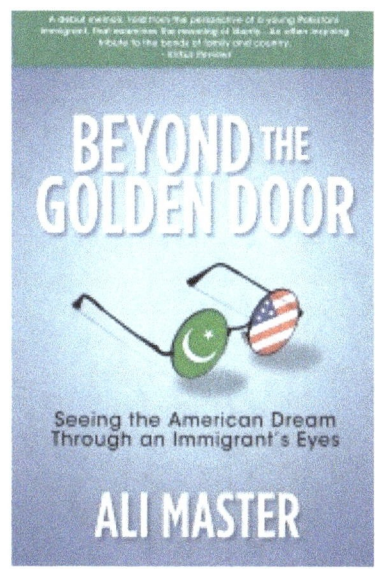

BEYOND THE GOLDEN DOOR
Ali Master

Reviewer: Jeyran Main

In *Beyond the Golden Door: Seeing the American Dream Through an Immigrant's Eyes,* Ali Master presents a deeply personal and reflective narrative of his experiences as a Pakistani Muslim who immigrated to the United States for college. Rather than providing an academic analysis of the nation's complex issues, Master offers an insightful and heartfelt perspective, shaped by his thirty-two years in the U.S. and additional years in three other countries. His central theme is that being American transcends ethnicity, religion, or skin color and is instead defined by shared values and freedoms.

The book is structured into four distinct parts. The first section delves into Master's upbringing in a devout Shia Muslim household in Pakistan. He provides a vivid depiction of Pakistani customs, politics, and cultural practices while also sharing the personal and traumatic experiences that have shaped his life. This section offers readers an intimate look at the foundations of his journey.

The book's second part transitions to a more humorous tone, featuring anecdotes about the stereotypes immigrants hold about American life and the reality of culture shock. Master's wit and ability to find humor in his cultural adjustments add a light-hearted dimension to his narrative, making it both engaging and entertaining.

In the third section, Master reflects on five American freedoms that he values deeply, offering a personal perspective on what these freedoms mean to him. This part highlights his appreciation for the principles that underpin the American experience. The final section poses contemplative questions for readers, encouraging them to reflect on their own beliefs and experiences.

Master's storytelling is both engaging and distinctive. His descriptions of Pakistani matchmaking and arranged marriages are handled with sensitivity and clarity, while his humorous observations about American stereotypes add charm to the narrative. The book is well-edited, with minimal profanity and a respectful approach to sensitive topics like sexual abuse.

Beyond the Golden Door is an inspiring and thought-provoking read that provides valuable insights into the immigrant experience and the true meaning of the American Dream. It is recommended for Muslims, Christians, immigrants, and anyone interested in exploring American identity and values.

SANDPEOPLE: AN ACROSS TIME MYSTERY
Cheryl Kerr

Reviewer: Jeyran Main

In *SandPeople: An Across Time Mystery*, Cheryl Kerr delivers a captivating coming-of-age story infused with history, mystery, and a touch of the supernatural. The novel follows twelve-year-old Lea McKinney, whose summer plans are upended when her parents announce their separation Lea must spend the season in Texas with an aunt she barely knows while her brother stays with their grandmother. Struggling with feelings of abandonment and frustration, Lea's summer promises to be challenging, filled with unfamiliar surroundings and the absence of her best friend, Laura.

Kerr crafts a narrative focusing on Lea's emotional journey rather than the specifics of her parents' separation. The story highlights Lea's growth as she adjusts to life with her aunt and learns to embrace her new environment. Through Lea's experiences, Kerr explores themes of personal growth and adaptation, demonstrating how one can make the best of circumstances beyond their control. The incorporation of historical fiction elements adds depth and excitement, blending seamlessly into the storyline without overshadowing the personal narrative.

The book is particularly engaging due to Kerr's vivid and imaginative writing. The summer setting comes alive through scenes such as horseback riding to an abandoned mission, searching for buried treasure with a metal detector, and exploring a life-size model ship. These adventurous elements create a vibrant backdrop that allows readers' imaginations to flourish. Kerr's depiction of Lea's transition from childhood to adolescence is relatable and poignant, capturing the essence of growing up and adjusting to unexpected changes.

The book is well-suited for upper middle-grade readers, with straightforward, age-appropriate content and minimal errors. Lea's journey is portrayed authentically, making her struggles and growth relatable for young readers. *SandPeople* is a delightful and engaging middle-grade novel that offers an enjoyable escape and a thoughtful reflection on navigating change. It is highly recommended for readers navigating their transitions or seeking an adventurous summer read.

Book Reviews

What a Tale My Thoughts Will Tell
Words Not to Be Forgotten
A Memoir of Happiness, Sorrow, Pain, and Regret

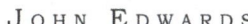

JOHN EDWARDS

WHAT A TALE MY THOUGHTS WILL TELL
John Edwards

Reviewer: Jeyran Main

In *What a Tale My Thoughts Will Tell*, John Edwards offers an elegant and profound exploration of life's unexpected twists and turns. The book delves into how life often diverges from our expectations, revealing the dual nature of transitions—some leading to dreams fulfilled and others resulting in trauma and disillusionment. Edwards, with his deep understanding of these experiences, invites readers into his personal odyssey, blending humor, vulnerability, and courage to discuss the impact of cultural, psychological, and sociological influences on our happiness and disappointments.

Edwards' narrative is a compelling mix of introspection and storytelling. He candidly recounts the highs of falling in love, the responsibilities of providing for a family, and the heartaches of infidelity, divorce, and estrangement. His exploration of these themes is marked by passion and empathy, making his experiences relatable and deeply moving.

A distinctive feature of the book is Edwards' use of musical songs and lyrics as a thematic thread and emotional vehicle. He writes, "Music binds us like language rarely does. Music is the window to the soul." This integration of music as a timeline and expressive tool enriches the narrative, offering a depth of emotional resonance that transcends mere words.

With the wisdom accrued from seventy years of life, Edwards presents a compassionate and insightful story that resonates with a wide range of human emotions. His reflections on his journey —from his origins and aspirations to the core dynamic that he believes defines the true meaning of life—are both thought-provoking and inspiring.

What a Tale My Thoughts Will Tell is not just a personal memoir but a universal exploration of life's complexities and the lessons they impart. It is a beautifully written, unforgettable book that will leave readers reflecting on their own experiences and the music that binds them.

THE IMPOSSIBLE MOCK ORANGE TRIAL
Thad G. Long

Reviewer: Jeyran Main

In *The Impossible Mock Orange Trial*, Thad G. Long presents a riveting legal thriller set in the small, racially and economically divided hamlet of Groveton, Phoenix County. The story begins with a tragic accident when Bess Johnson, borrowing a van from her sheriff uncle, crashes into a symbolic mock orange tree—a stark reminder of the region's painful history of slavery. The crash results in the death of young Serena Miller and severe injury to Jimason, while Bess and the others suffer minor injuries.

Long's novel intricately explores the accident's aftermath through the lens of a high-stakes legal battle. The plaintiffs, a group of small-town African Americans grappling with racial and economic hardships, seek a substantial payout from the large corporations involved, namely Universal Tire Company and Tergano Motor Corporation. The challenge is formidable, given Phoenix County's reputation for favoring locals and the complex legal issues at play.

The narrative unfolds with a detailed examination of the legal process, focusing on the tension between the plaintiffs' hope for justice and the defendants' efforts to prove their case. The investigation reveals potential design flaws in the van and highlights various factors, including Bess's inexperience with the vehicle and the poor condition of its tire. The story is enriched by the dynamic between the defense team led by Ted Born and Dave Thompson, who strive for a fair trial despite personal conflicts and the hostile legal environment.

Long's descriptive and well-paced writing draws readers into the intricacies of the trial. His legal background adds authenticity to the portrayal of courtroom drama, while his skillful characterization makes the emotional and socio-economic stakes palpable. The book is a compelling page-turner, with minimal jargon and accessible language that exposes the flaws in the judicial system while reaffirming its potential for justice.

The novel's engaging plot, rich character development, and unexpected twists keep readers hooked until the final verdict. Despite a few minor errors, the book is expertly edited and deserving of high praise. It is recommended for readers who enjoy legal thrillers with a strong human element and mature themes. *The Impossible Mock Orange Trial* is a standout addition to the genre and a must-read for those captivated by the complexities of justice and human resilience.

NEITHER SAFE NOR EFFECTIVE (2ND EDITION) BY DR. COLLEEN HUBER

Governments in Europe and North America have released data on COVID-19 vaccines' effects on people who took them. Screenshots of those pages back up the material in this book.

Are the COVID-19 vaccines safe?

Do they meet the Bradford Hill causation criteria regarding reported health events following the vaccines?

What happened in the Pfizer study?

What happened in the animal studies?

Colleen Huber, NMD, is a Naturopathic Medical Doctor and medical expert witness in court cases related to vaccine safety concerns and events. To prepare testimony for court cases, Dr. Huber cites and compiles vital statistics and other data from governments around the US and the world, as well as data from vaccine manufacturers.

Please make sure you have all of the available and relevant information on the COVID vaccines before your final decision is made.

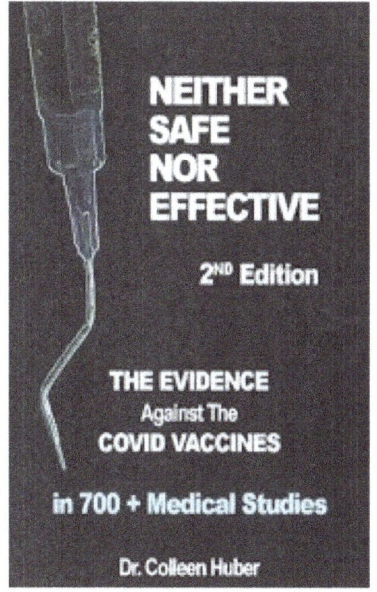

LAUNCHPAD REPUBLIC BY HOWARD WOLK, JOHN LANDRY

In *Launchpad Republic: America's Entrepreneurial Edge and Why it Matters to All of Us*, Howard Wolk and John Landry delve into the rich history of American entrepreneurship. They explore how the nation's political, legal, and cultural frameworks have nurtured innovation and "creative destruction" for over 200 years. The book reveals the unique attributes that have set America apart from other countries and discusses the essential qualities needed to sustain its leadership in the future.

The authors highlight how America's democratic system allows new companies to challenge established ones, driving robust start-up activity and continuous improvement among large corporations. This dynamic environment encourages investment and innovation, contrasting sharply with other models like Europe's consensus-driven approach and China's authoritarian system.

Launchpad Republic offers a thorough examination of how America's history has shaped its economic landscape, addressing contemporary challenges such as Big Tech, inequality, and stakeholder capitalism. Written in an engaging style, the book is a valuable read for anyone interested in understanding the forces that have influenced—and will continue to influence—America's entrepreneurial spirit and economic trajectory.